Characteristics and Traits That Make Up a Strong Church

Characteristics and Traits That Make Up a Strong Church

Byron Calhoun

J. Kenkade
PUBLISHING®

Little Rock, Arkansas

J. Kenkade Publishing

6104 Forbing Rd

Little Rock, AR 72209

www.jkenkadepublishing.com

Facebook.com/jkenkadepublishing

J. Kenkade Publishing is a registered trademark.

Printed in the United States of America

ISBN 978-1-955186-25-4

DEDICATION

In loving memory of my uncle, Alvin Tate. Also, I would like to thank my wife, Santisha Calhoun, and my children, Layla Calhoun, Kaci Calhoun, and Byron "Cal" Calhoun Jr.

To GOD be the glory for the great things HE has done. Stay focused.

Contents

WE MUST BE A CHURCH OF FAITH

—❧—

A. What is FAITH? (Hebrews 11)

- Faith *knocks down* the **barriers of unbelief**.

- Faith *pushes you* into your **destination**.

- Faith *proves you* to **yourself**.

- Faith *never makes sense*; it is the act of possibility after impossibility.

- Faith is **abnormal thinking/believing**.

B. Different LEVELS OF FAITH (Romans 12:3, Measure of FAITH)

- "Faith the size..." (Matthew 17:20-22)

- "Believe and not doubt..." (James 1:6)

- "You of *little faith*..." (Matthew 8:26)

C. Different TYPES OF FAITH

- Sustaining FAITH

- That <u>thinking</u> faith should shift to <u>doing</u> faith (James 2:14-26, Hebrews 10:23, Romans 4:20-21).

- Surviving FAITH (Luke 8:22-25, Matthew 14:22-33)

- Growing FAITH (2 Thess. 1:2-3)

- Great "crazy" FAITH

- There is a difference between *faith* and *ignorance.*

Ignorance is believing something to be true that isn't.

Foolishness is the lack of good sense or judgement; stupidity.

> **~ Martin Luther King Jr.** stated, "Faith is taking the first step even when you don't see the whole staircase."

> **~Bob Proctor** stated, "Faith and fear both demand you believe in something you cannot see. You choose."

> **~Rick Warren** stated, "Fear is a self-imposed prison that will keep you from becoming what GOD intends for you to be. You must move against it with the weapons of faith and love."

Faith, to those who believe, should be so *powerful* that it appears *ignorant* and *foolish* to the nonbeliever. It could possibly even cause a believer to scratch their head and between imagination and the possibility of reality. The slightest form of doubt could possibly delay your request.

Chapter

WE MUST BE A CHURCH OF CONSISTENCY

There are different ways to ensure that you remain consistent. Disregard negative influence, disregard doubt, keep paper, pen/pencil, plan, and a promise to yourself.

A. **DO NOT just be CONSISTENT in normal CHRIST-less ROUTINE (Acts 3:1-11).**

- In other words, be consistent in something worthwhile, such as your study, exercise, diet, path to goals, and time (1 Cor. 15:58).

Being inconsistent in time can keep you in a state of always saying what you are *about* to do because you disregarded your "now"… so "later" never comes.

B. CONSISTENCY   produces   POSITIVE DEDICATION

- Consistency eventually leads to dedication, dedication leads to success, and success leads to being successful.

- "If you are persistent, you will get it. If you are consistent, you will keep it." – Anonymous

C. GOD is CONSISTENT in WHO HE is (Malachi 3:6, Psalm 102:27, Numbers 23:19, Titus 1:2, Hebrews 13:8).

- "I am the LORD, I change not." (Malachi 3:6)

- "JESUS CHRIST the same yesterday, and to day, and for ever." (Hebrews 13:8).

  o GOD has been <u>consistent</u> in *forgiving* us.

  o GOD has been <u>consistent</u> in *keeping* us.

  o GOD has been <u>consistent</u> in *walking* with us.

  o GOD is <u>consistent</u> in *covering* us.

  o GOD is <u>consistent</u> in *providing* for us.

  o GOD is <u>consistent</u> in *leading* us.

  o GOD is <u>consistent</u> in *loving* us.

  o GOD is <u>consistent</u> in *making* ways for us.

  o GOD is <u>consistent</u> in *maintaining* us.

D. Consistency REVEALS the DRIVE in others.

- When we are consistent ourselves, it will allow us to see what's in others. "Real recognize real", as they say.

12

o You will know what *drive* looks like because you possess it!

o You will know what *push* looks like because you possess it!

o You will know what an *excuse* is because it will be strange to your vocabulary.

o You will know the importance of not walking away from *ministry* because something didn't go your way.

• Thomas Edison said it like this: "Our greatest weakness lies in giving up. The most certain way to succeed is *always* to try just one more time."

• Anonymous said, "I refuse to quit because I haven't tried all possible ways yet."

• Nelson Mandela said, "I never lose. I either win or I learn."

E. **Be consistent in your *belief* (Daniel 6:10, Titus 2:7-8).**

3

WE MUST BE A CHURCH OF LOVE

A. Love is a must amongst us as believers. It is vital and important (1 John 4:7-16). <u>Do not get love and lust mixed up.</u>

- **<u>Love</u>** is an intense feeling of deep affection. **<u>Lust</u>** is very strong sexual desire. Love deals with matters of the **heart**. Lust deals with matters of the **flesh**.

- Thinking with your heart can pruduce different results than thinking in the flesh.

- JESUS always responded in love. HE even forgave while on the cross.

- We love because our leader was full of love. He, being full of love, should let us as believers know that HE does not do anything to harm us in longevity but to help us for eternity!

- His display of harsh love (whoopings, punishment, heartache, etc) is for a helping lesson.

- Pastor Charles Carradine says that love is the bar in our closet that everything else hangs on (Matthew 22:37-40).

- "Hatred stirreth up strife: but love covert all sins." (Proverbs 10:12)

- "So now faith, hope, and *love* abide, these three; but the greatest of these is *love*." (1Corinthians 13:13)

- "Let all that you do be done in *love*." (1 Corinthians 16:14)

- In reference to the *power* of *love*, Dr. Seuss said, "You know you are in *love* when you can't fall asleep because the reality is finally better than your dreams."

- "And above all these put on *love*, which binds *everything together* in *perfect harmony*." (Colossians 3:14)

- Rupi Kaur says, "How you *love* yourself is how you teach others to *love* you."

- Love causes you to turn the other cheek. Love causes you to treat your neighbor different than the negative treatment they give/show you. Love heals. Love produces/breeds positivity. Love must be *inward* ("If any is in CHRIST he is a new creature" – 2 Cor. 5:17). Our identity, character, and attitude change when we really get in HIM and allow HIM to reside in us.

- You should love you enough not to lose you trying to find good or fault in others. **Suicidal thoughts** can be traced to an issue with inner love, **Heathy (fitness)**

lifestyles say a lot about how you treat yourself. Personal thoughts such as **Jealousy** can be traced back to how you feel about yourself.

- Loving yourself, having faith in yourself, encouraging yourself builds *courage* and *confidence* in yourself.

- To have a lack of *confidence* is to have a Lack of *love within*, and the less *confident* you are in *self*, the more *you see others as a threat*. You begin to dissect who they are and wonder how they got where they are, how did they achieve that, did they really deserve that.

- Loving yourself allows you to see the *good and positive* in others.

- Loving yourself concerning relationships allows you to *love* others in a way they deserve to be *loved*. Loving yourself is an *indication* to others that they can take a chance with you because they have seen how you treat yourself.

- Single children sometimes have a problem with loving or sharing with others because they grew up by themselves.

- **Horizontal** – You can't love GOD and hate your brother (Proverbs 19:8, Mark 12:31, 1 John 4:20).

  o Love is the *key factor* or *force* behind other spiritual matters that can hinder our Christian walk, such as: forgiveness, marital matters, family matters (court proceedings).

- **Vertical** – 1 John 4:16-19, 21.

  o "Love is the cure for a multitude of sins." (Peter 4:8)

- **Four Types of Love**

  o Ellen Mcgrath published an article on December 1, 2002, in *Psychology Today* entitled, "The Power of Love."

  o Love is as critical for your mind and body as oxygen. It's not negotiable. The more connected you are, the healthier you will be both physically and emotionally. The less connected you are, the more you are at risk.

  o It is also true that the less love you have, the more **depression** you are likely to experience in your life. Love is probably the best **antidepressant** there is because one of the most common sources of depression is feeling unloved. Most depressed people don't love themselves, and they do not feel loved by others. They also are very self-focused, making them less attractive to others and depriving them of opportunities to learn the skills of love.

  o Most of us get our ideas of love from popular culture. We come to believe that love is something that sweeps us off our feet. But the pop-culture ideal of love consists of unrealistic images created for entertainment, which is one reason so many of us are set up to be depressed. It's part of our national vulnerability, like eating junk food. We're constantly stimulated by images of instant gratification. We think it is love when it's simply distraction and infatuation.

o   One consequence is that when we hit real love we become upset and disappointed because there are many things that do not fit the cultural ideal. Some of us get demanding and controlling, wanting someone else to do what we think our ideal of romance should be, without realizing our ideal is misplaced.

Chapter

WE MUST BE A CHURCH OF PRAYER

❧

A. Prayer is a vital part of a believer's life and one of the connection pieces to connect with the LORD. It is a form of communication, request, plea, and thankfulness. Prayer builds our bond with the Father; any relationship that is strong and built on trust involves communication. This type of communication is not and should not be one way... but it is a devotional-driven dialogue with the Divine.

This is the reality: <u>What HE has to say is more important than what we have to say.</u>

Jeremiah 29:11-12 says, "For I know the thoughts that I think towards you, saith the LORD, thoughts of Peace, and not of evil, to give you an expected end. Then shall ye call upon me, and ye shall go and pray unto me and I will hearken unto you."

That word "hearken" comes from the Hebrew word "shama", meaning to *hear, listen to, and obey*. See, saints, contrary to popular belief, there is a big difference between *hearing* and *listening*.

Merriam-Webster defines **hearing** as "the process, function, or power of perceiving sound; specifically: the special sense by which noises and tones are received as stimuli."

Listening, on the other hand, means "to pay attention to sound; to hear something with thoughtful attention; and to give consideration."

In other words, GOD will not just hear your sound by recognizing your voice, but HE will zoom into your voice that has caught HIM attention and carefully dissect your dialogue so that HE can later obey your request.

John 1:1-14 displays to us the gospel of the trinity. This is where we now find the privilege in prayer to our GOD. We no longer have to go confess to a priest, but we now have direct access to the Divine. These scriptures show that the Word has now become flesh. Understand that since our LORD and Savior JESUS CHRIST is trinity, HE can be GOD and still pray to GOD because while they may share the same being, they are different in person.

Each person of the trinity plays a different role in how they interact in the lives of believers and unbelievers alike. When it comes to our given topic of prayer, the Bible teaches that it is GOD the Father to whom we ought to direct our prayers, but it also teaches that it is through JESUS that we have that kind of direct access to the Father. Consider Mark 15:38 – "And the curtain of the temple was torn in two, from top to bottom." This "curtain" is the one that separated people from the Holy of Holies (AKA "The Most Holy Place") in the temple, the place where GOD's presence dwelled in a special sense. The Holy of Holies was the place where once a year a priest would enter after having carefully observed all of the purification rituals that were required before entering into GOD's presence and make a sacrifice for the unintentional sins of the people of Israel (intentional or known sins were to be dealt with on a regular basis). The curtain was torn in two by GOD at the time of JESUS' death on the cross. Hebrews 9:1-14 tells us that through CHRIST'S death we no longer are separated from GOD by the curtain.

Plainly put, <u>one other reason we pray is because HE prayed</u>. That's why the songwriter says, "What a *friend* we have in *JESUS*, all our sins and griefs. What a *privilege* it is to carry *everything to GOD in prayer*."

- JESUS prayed. There is power in prayer.

  o The power in prayer is not a power that comes from the *act* of prayer. It is a power that flows from the One to whom we pray. In our impotent humanity, we are blessed to be able to reach upward to GOD in prayer knowing that HE hears. In HIS omnipotence, HE responds, and we receive – that's the power of prayer! Prayer unleashes a deeper communion with GOD in our hearts, and it comforts our souls. It grows within us a richer faith in who HE is and unleashes power in us to live our lives in service to HIM and others. The power is not in our petition. The power comes from HIS response and a confidence in knowing HE is ever-present with us.

o   "And whatsoever ye shall ask in my name, that will I do, that the Father may be glorified in the Son." (John 14:13-14)

o   "And this is the confidence that we have in HIM that, if we ask any thing according to HIS will, HE heareth us..." (1 John 5:14-15)

o   "If any of you lack wisdom, let him ask of GOD, that giveth to all [men] liberally, and upbraideth not; and it shall be given him." (James 1:5)

o   "The effectual fervent prayer of a righteous man availeth much." (James 5:16)

Effectual: producing or able to produce a desired effect.

What does "fervent" mean in the Bible?

Fervent: having or showing great warmth or intensity of spirit, feeling, enthusiasm, etc.; ardent: a **fervent** admirer; a **fervent** plea. hot; burning; glowing.

o   "And I say unto you, Ask, and it shall be given you; seek, and ye shall find; knock, and it shall be opened unto you." (Luke 11:9)

o **Forms of Prayer**

The tradition of the Roman Catholic Church highlights **four** basic types of prayer:

1. The prayer of blessing and adoration.
2. The prayer of petition.
3. The prayer of intercession.
4. The prayer of thanksgiving.

Prayer shows up all throughout the Bible. If prayer is heartfelt conversation with GOD, then we find it as early as Adam's interactions with GOD in the garden of Eden. We also see it as late as the prayer for JESUS CHRIST to return again in glory at the end of the book of Revelation. There are countless examples of individuals offering up prayers to GOD within the Bible. And there is a whole book of the Bible – the Psalms – that is made up entirely of prayers.

One of the consistent themes in the New Testament's teaching about prayer is that we can be assured that GOD will hear and respond to our prayers. The apostle John points to this when he says, "This is the confidence we have in approaching GOD: that if we ask anything according to HIS will, HE hears us" (1 John 5:14, NIV). This is a wonderful message! It tells us that GOD knows our needs and that GOD absolutely expects us to bring our needs to HIM through prayer.

One way to think about prayer in the Bible is to look at the different types of prayers that we find. Perhaps the easiest way to think about the major biblical modes of prayer is through the acronym "ACTS". It stands for Adoration, Confession, Thanksgiving, and Supplication. The four types of prayer that go by these names are found in many places in the Bible.

o **Prayers of Adoration**

A prayer of adoration is a prayer that praises GOD's goodness and majesty. In the Bible, we find prayers of adoration in the Psalms, which are often called psalms of praise.

For instance, Psalm 111:1-14 (NRSV):

"Praise the LORD!I will give thanks to the LORD with my whole heart,in the company of the upright, in the congregation.Great are the works of the LORD,studied by all who delight in them.Full of honor and majesty is HIS work,and HIS righteousness endures forever.HE has gained renown by HIS wonderful deeds;the LORD is gracious and merciful."

Psalm 18:1 –

"For the choir director. A Psalm of David the servant of the LORD, who spoke to the LORD the words of this song in the day that the LORD delivered him from the hand of all his enemies and from the hand of Saul. And he said, "I love You, O LORD, my strength."

Psalm 26:8 –

"O LORD, I love the habitation of YOUR house

And the place where YOUR glory dwells."

Psalm 5:7 –

"But as for me, by Your abundant lovingkindness I will enter Your house,

At Your holy temple I will bow in reverence for You."

Exodus 3:5 –

"Then HE said, 'Do not come near here; remove your sandals from your feet, for the place on which you are standing is holy ground.'"

Deuteronomy 13:4 –

"You shall follow the LORD your GOD and fear HIM; and you shall keep HIS commandments, listen to HIS voice, serve HIM, and cling to HIM."

Joshua 5:15 –

"The captain of the LORD's host said to Joshua, 'Remove your sandals from your feet, for the place where you are standing is holy.' And Joshua did so."

1 Chronicles 16:29 –

"Ascribe to the LORD the glory due HIS name;

Bring an offering, and come before HIM;

Worship the LORD in holy array."

Psalm 29:2 –

"Ascribe to the LORD the glory due to HIS name;

Worship the LORD in holy array."

Psalm 33:8 –

"Let all the earth fear the LORD;

Let all the inhabitants of the world stand in awe of HIM."

Psalm 95:6 –

"Come, let us worship and bow down,

Let us kneel before the LORD our Maker."

Psalm 99:5 –

"Exalt the LORD our GOD

And worship at HIS footstool;

Holy is He."

o **Prayers of Confession**

A prayer of confession is a searching prayer of the heart. When we confess, we bare our souls before GOD about our sins and shortcomings. Confession to GOD is also a model for the kind of mutual confession that believers in the body of CHRIST are called upon to make to one another (see James 5:16). But ultimately, since all sin is sin against GOD, we are called to confess our sins to GOD. A key part of the good news of JESUS is that repentance can bring forgiveness and new life. Indeed, the Bible assures us that sincere confession before GOD will be met with forgiveness. We see this in 1 John 1:9 (NRSV), which says, "If we confess our sins, HE who is faithful and just will forgive us our sins and cleanse us from all unrighteousness."

So prayers of confession ought to be a regular part of our spiritual lives, as we become transformed into the people GOD would have us be.

"Therefore confess your sins to each other and pray for each other so that you may be healed. The prayer of a righteous person is powerful and effective." (James 5:16, NIV)

"If we confess our sins, HE is faithful and just and will forgive us our sins and purify us from all unrighteousness." (1 John 1:9, NIV)

"Whoever conceals their sins does not prosper,but the one who confesses and renounces them finds mercy." (Proverbs 28:13, NIV)

"Then I acknowledged my sin to youand did not cover up my iniquity.I said, 'I will confess my transgressions to the LORD.'And you forgave the guilt of my sin." (Psalm 32:5, NIV)

"When anyone becomes aware that they are guilty in any of these matters, they must confess in what way they have sinned." (Leviticus 5:5, NIV)

"Repent, then, and turn to GOD, so that your sins may be wiped out, that times of refreshing may come from the LORD." (Acts 3:19, NIV)

"For it is with your heart that you believe and are justified, and it is with your mouth that you profess your faith and are saved." (Romans 10:10, NIV)

"When I kept silent, my bones wasted away through my

groaning all day long." (Psalm 32:3, NIV)

"Come near to GOD and HE will come near to you. Wash your hands, you sinners, and purify your hearts, you double-minded." (James 4:8, NIV)

"We have sinned and done wrong. We have been wicked and have rebelled; we have turned away from your commands and laws." (Daniel 9:5, NIV)

"For all have sinned and fall short of the glory of GOD, and all are justified freely by HIS grace through the redemption that came by CHRIST JESUS." (Romans 3:23-24, NIV)

"If you declare with your mouth, 'JESUS is LORD,' and believe in your heart that GOD raised him from the dead, you will be saved." (Romans 10:9, NIV)

o **Prayers of Thanksgiving**

A prayer of thanksgiving is a prayer that recognizes the good things GOD gives us and offers thanks for them: our lives, our health, our families, and our faith. The apostle Paul told us, "Rejoice always, pray without ceasing, give thanks in all circumstances; for this is the will of GOD in CHRIST JESUS for you" (1 Thess. 5:16-18, NRSV). A part of what it means to live faithfully is to live out of a deep sense of gratitude for all that GOD has done for us. Prayers of thanksgiving help us to do that. They give proper thanks to GOD and also shape us into thankful people at our core.

• "Give thanks to the LORD, for HE is good; HIS love endures forever." (1 Chronicles 16:34)

- "Let the peace of CHRIST rule in your hearts, since as members of one body you were called to peace. And be thankful." (Colossians 3:15)

- "Devote yourselves to prayer, being watchful and thankful." (Colossians 4:2)

- "I always thank my GOD for you because of HIS grace given you in CHRIST JESUS." (1 Corinthians 1:4)

- "You will be enriched in every way so that you can be generous on every occasion, and through us your generosity will result in thanksgiving to GOD." (2 Corinthians 9:11)

- "For everything GOD created is good, and nothing is to be rejected if it is received with thanksgiving, because it is consecrated by the word of GOD and prayer." (1 Timothy 4:4-5)

- "Rejoice always, pray continually, give thanks in all circumstances; for this is GOD's will for you in CHRIST JESUS." (1 Thess. 5:16-18)

- "Do not be anxious about anything, but in every situation, by prayer and petition, with thanksgiving, present your requests to GOD. And the peace of GOD, which transcends all understanding, will guard your hearts and your minds in CHRIST JESUS." (Philippians 4:6-7)

- "But I, with shouts of grateful praise, will sacrifice to you. What I have vowed I will make good. I will say, 'Salvation comes from the LORD.'" (Jonah 2:9)

- "The LORD is my strength and my shield; in HIM my heart trusts, and I am helped; my heart exults, and with my song I give thanks to HIM." (Psalm 28:7)

- "Offer to GOD a sacrifice of thanksgiving, and perform your vows to the Most High." (Psalm 50:14)

o **Prayers of Supplication**

A prayer of supplication is a prayer that lifts up requests before GOD. Supplications are often divided between those requests we make for ourselves (petitions) and those requests we make on behalf of other people (intercessions). We can turn again to the apostle Paul, who told us in Philippians 4:6 (NRSV), "Do not worry about anything, but with prayer and supplication with thanksgiving let your requests be made known to GOD." It is natural for us to ask GOD for the desires of our hearts, and we can be assured that GOD will answer our prayers. Just so, we feel the need to pray on behalf of others as well—our family and friends, as well as those whose needs we know even if we do not know them personally. GOD does answer prayer, even if we need to be mindful that GOD's answers to prayer are not always the answers we want GOD to give!

Prayer is a vessel to allow us to gain more **knowledge**.

Prayer causes a stormy atmosphere to become **calm**.

Prayer causes us to stand **firm** and **confident** against the devil and demons.

There is a misconception about prayer we must look at. There is a difference between prayer always working and prayer always changing things. Prayer always works, but prayer does not always change. In regard to prayer always working, we must admit that the communication line is always accessible because HIS silence is still a form of an answer. But just because you pray, it does not necessarily mean that it will work out your way. In other words, you can always pray, but that doesn't mean that HE is obligated to give you exactly what you pray for.

Malachi 3:6 reads, "For I am the LORD, I change not." So maybe this ought to allow us to see prayer from a different angle or more mature stance. Many of us pray to change GOD's will while we remain the same or change HIS mind to conform to us when maybe we ought to pray to better understand HIS will, discover HIS will, accept HIS will, and do HIS will. Simply stated, we should pray for our hearts and minds to accept what GOD allows.

Luke 12:7 and Matthew 10:30 declare that even the very hairs of your head are numbered.

GOD knows all. You cannot psych HIM out. Even if you prayed and HE changed HIS mind, it was probably already in HIS will.

Now let's discuss Psalms 20:4 and Psalms 37:4:

"Grant thee according to thine own heart, and fulfill all the counsel." (Psalms 20:4)

"Delight (please greatly....high degree of gratification or pleasure) thyself also in the LORD; and HE shall give thee the desires of thine heart. Commit thy way unto the

LORD; **trust** also in HIM and HE shall bring it to pass."
(Psalms 37:4-5)

So now the question becomes: How is John so *confident* about
the results of prayer in 1 John 5:14-15? John understood
that GOD is light, GOD is love, and GOD is life.

John had a strong desire and fellowship with GOD. John
knew that if GOD is a GOD of light, then HE cannot
walk in darkness. And one way to stay out of the darkness
is to confess our sins to the LORD and allow HIS blood to
cleanse us. In other words, many of us approach GOD with
endless requests when we should approach HIM with our
confessions. Sincere confession will release the darkness of
sin so that GOD can give us our blessing.

John also knew that GOD is a GOD of love. Love is more
than merely words; love is action, and love is giving. Love
is dealing with matters of the heart. GOD is a Giver. HE
wants nothing more but to be a Giver and a Blesser. But
we cannot treat HIM like trash and expect HIM to give us
treasure as we remain the same. John also knew that GOD
is life.

Plainly put, the results of prayer are sometimes predicated
on your alignment with the Father.

Discussion on the LORD's Prayer can be found in Matthew
6:5-15, 9-13 and Luke 11:1-13

"Our Father which art in heaven" means we're
praying to our Heavenly Father who lives in heaven. GOD
likes it when we call HIM Father, and HE wants us to talk to

HIM just like we talk to our own fathers. GOD is our loving Father, and we are HIM special children.

"Hallowed be thy name" means GOD's name is holy and special. Even though GOD wants us to call HIM our Father, HE is still GOD, and HE is to be respected and honored.

"Thy kingdom come. Thy will be done on earth, as it is in heaven." If we think about where GOD lives, we know it's pretty great. The Bible says that in heaven there will be no more crying, GOD will live with us, and there will be no hunger or hurt there. This part of the prayer says to let GOD's kingdom come and let GOD's will be done on Earth, both just like it is in heaven. This means we are praying that people would live in peace and love one another, the way it is in heaven. It reminds us that we should be living the way GOD wants us to every day.

"Give us this day our daily bread" means give us today all that we really need. Keep in mind that these are things that we can't live without. We don't need video games and princess dolls to survive. Those are the things that we want; we need food, water, and shelter. We ask GOD to provide for us because we love and trust HIM.

"And forgive us our debts, as we forgive our debtors." This next part of the prayer is asking for forgiveness for our mistakes. Forgiveness means that we are sorry for something we've done and we don't want to do it anymore. But we also need to forgive people who have done wrong to us. Sometimes others hurt us very badly, so we need to ask GOD to help us forgive them. If we forgive others, GOD will forgive us.

"And lead us not into temptation, but deliver us from evil." It is sometimes very tempting to do something you're not supposed to. This part is really neat because it asks GOD to help us to know the right thing to do, protect us against the evil that is in the world, and keep us away from it.

"For thine is the kingdom, and the power, and the glory, forever. Amen." The last part of the prayer is the best part! "For Yours is the kingdom" means that Heaven will last forever and will always be GOD. GOD also has all the power and all the glory <u>forever</u>! It makes me happy knowing that GOD will never die and He's the strongest and greatest. With GOD, we will always win! "Amen" means "So be it." We are asking for this to be the way things are.

Chapter

WE MUST BE A CHURCH OF VISION, MISSION, PLANNING, AND PURPOSE

❧

A. I believe that <u>vision</u> has to be <u>planned</u> out for other to understand it. What is <u>planned</u> becomes our <u>mission</u>. Our <u>mission</u> then becomes our <u>purpose</u>.... Our "why" and our purpose are the reference points to who we are or why we exist.

Vision, mission, and purpose should go further than your normal thinking. They should *stretch* and create a place of *discomfort* in regard to making sure the *mission* is complete. In order to make sure it is done, you must have *proper planning*.

o   What is your "why"?

o   What is your identity? What are you known for?

o   What is the fingerprint of your mission?

o   What is your accountability for yourself?

o   Who in your circle is accountable for you on days when you want to give up on yourself?

o   Do the people in your circle or team really have your best interest in mind?

DEFINITIONS

Vision: the faculty or state of being able to see.

Visionary: person thinking about or planning the future with imagination or wisdom

Trust the visionary due to the fact that what he or she is putting out will more than likely not make any sense to others. The present budget won't match the future plan, which means it will also take *prayer* and *faith* ("crazy" faith; see lesson on faith). It is also vital for the visionary to have a team that understands his or her ignorance. The reason I use the word "ignorance" is because until *total trust* is built for the visionary, that's how others will perceive them. Vision is not supposed to make sense. A vision also keeps you *focused* on the "overall plan" without void, over-relaxation, stagnancy, and too much time remaining idle. A brand-new car that sits still too long will create problems because it is designed to move and transport.

Vision is nerve-racking and can be scary! It's up to you to make it work. Vision is the forward-thinking thoughts that fit your identity and overall purpose.

Question for further study: Why is vision so important? Mark 8:22-26 will show us the difference between **sight** and **vision**.

Vision: the overall/complete goal or what is seen spiritually to be achieved or accomplished. (Or is all vision spiritual?)

Planning: what it takes to strategize and to make sure you do not detour from the process.

o "And let us not grow weary of doing good, for in due season we will reap, **if we do not give up**." (Galatians 6:9, ESV)

o "And afterward, I will pour out my Spirit on all people. Your sons and daughters will prophesy, your old men will dream dreams, your young men will see visions." (Joel 2:28)

This scripture is important to us because at one point, the spirit was there.

This lets us know that there is a difference between *dreams* and *visions*. Or is there? One might happen during sleep, while the other may happen while we are awake.

Note of importance: GOD is a GOD of Revelation. HIS Word and work will be revealed if HE wants them to be. HE is sovereign enough to speak and or reveal HIMSELF in many different ways. GOD has come in the form of bread, a cloud, fire at night, water, a lamb, the Good Shepherd, and so on.

It is my personal belief that GOD gives visions and dreams to reveal HIMSELF or HIS plan.

Psalm 37:4-5 lets us know that we shouldn't be faithful to a vision just because it's ours, but we should fulfill it because it came from GOD, which reverts it back to a matter of obedience.

So there is a process to the promises.

We first have to *delight* before HE gives us the *desires*. We first have to *commit* and *trust* before HE brings them to pass. There will always be a process to the promise. Moses had a *process* before the *promised land*.

Delight: to please someone greatly. Our job and focus is to please GOD and make HIM smile (Galatians 1:10, Eph. 6:6, 1 Thess. 2:4).

Desire: the craving, longing, and yearning. It suggests feelings that compel one toward the attainment or possession of something. Desire is a strong feeling, worthy or unworthy, that compels someone toward the attainment or possession of something that is (in reality or imagination) within reach: a desire for success.

Commit in verse 5 means "to roll" – roll away, roll down, as to suggest rolling away something very heavy like a burden (see also Matt.11:28-30, "come unto Me").

Habakkuk 2:2-3 says, "And the LORD answered me, and said, 'Write the vision, and make it plain upon tables, that he may run that readeth it. For the vision is yet for an appointed time, but at the end it shall speak, and not lie: though it tarry, wait for it; because it will surely come, it will not tarry.'"

In the book of Habakkuk, we are dealing with a stubborn nation that refuses to change its sinful ways. Habakkuk questions the wisdom of GOD. GOD allows the Babylonian empire to execute judgement on Judah for its sins.

Let's break down the scripture:

"The LORD answered me and said" – This is a responding Father (a response to verse 1 and prior verses).

"*Write the vision*" – Write it down because, later on, what you're pregnant with will benefit others. As a visionary, you cannot make someone else see something that you are blind to. When it is in writing, you have a visual aid that also serves as a visual reminder.

"*Make it plain*" – You are the carrier of the vision, but if others will benefit from it, they must understand it. You might have to write it down many different ways, explain it different ways, meet in smaller groups, and so on.

"*That he may run*" – The benefit of the vision to others is to strengthen them in making it practical. Running consists of keeping a pace beyond walking, swift movement, progress. Any time you run and utilize this form of energy, fatigue can set in. Teamwork is of great importance. Understand that the person who is running is the person who just heard the vision, which means he is running with joy, happiness, and an elated heart because he now has privileged information that can be a blessing to someone else.

It was also common practice in that day to write the writings big enough or with characters large enough so that if someone were running by, they could still read it and absorb it without stopping.

Isaiah 6:1-4 provides us with a very well-painted vision of heaven and heavenly personnel. Isaiah words it as if we were there. He says, "I saw the LORD sitting upon a throne, high and lifted up, and HIS train filled the temple."

o "Saw" – The LORD was visible.

o "Throne" – The LORD was seated and elevated high by consistent worship.

41

o   The train signified majesty, authority, and power. The longer it was denoted to the Sovereignty of the King.

o   Creatures were created for worship.

Can our eyes really grasp the greatness of HIM? Do our feet deserve to walk in HIS trail, in the magnitude of HIS matchless divinity and potent power of HIS presence seems unworthy of our humanness. We need to express consistent moving worship – nonstop verbal worship.

Revelation 1:9-20 reveals CHRIST, the love for HIS Church, and the leaders.

Mission: values of a company, organization, or individual.

In other words, the "mission" is basically what you are trying to accomplish.

Where is your destination for you and others? We will use Matthew 28:19-20 as a guide through this portion of study.

Planning/Plan: detailed proposal for doing or achieving something.

Your plan is your personal/organizational guide that is designed for you to stay on track and pace yourself and/or your team.

Question for further study: Are you in GOD's plan? What is your plan? What are the details of a planning process? What does it aim to?

We will look at the plan Paul had for Timothy. We will observe how Noah stuck to his plan concerning the arc.

Purpose – What is your "why"? Why does this organization need you? What is your central theme of motivation that makes you push harder than everyone to accomplish this task? Your purpose should always have goals attached to it, but you will have to have influence, not negative persuasion.

My definition of "influence" is maintaining a positive aura, speech, demeanor, and spirit about yourself that can rub off on others.

Negative persuasion comes off as coercion. It is my belief that that positive persuasion is important when it's done the right way. (This is my stance/opinion.)

Positive persuasion is encouragement at its best when others can't see what they possess or what your organization/ministry needs.

Question for further study: What is GOD's purpose for us? What is the purpose for yourself?

We will look at the Genesis account and the Creation of man.

Why is purpose important or necessary? Let's use the example of opening up a restaurant. Your purpose will keep you in alignment with your goals and necessities to reach your purpose.

Chapter

6

WE MUST BE A CHURCH OF SERVERS AND DOERS

A. "For even the Son of Man did not come to be served, but to serve, and to give HIS life as a ransom for many." (Mark 10:45)

o   Being a great server is about one simple principle: treat others the way you would like to be treated.

o   What makes you a good server?

Food servers must be cheerful and friendly, no matter how stressed, tired, or frustrated you may be. You may be responsible for fifteen tables at once. But your customers should feel that you care for them individually. Their dining experience depends on you staying positive and friendly.

Philippians 2:5-8 – These scriptures exposes the "attitude of CHRIST".

"⁵ Let this mind be in you, which was also in CHRIST JESUS:

⁶ Who, being in the form of GOD, thought it not robbery to be equal with GOD:

⁷ But made HIMSELF of no reputation, and took upon HIM the form of a servant, and was made in the likeness of men:

⁸ And being found in fashion as a man, HE humbled HIMSELF, and became obedient unto death, even the death of the cross."

21 Server Tips and Tricks

Here's a list of time-tested serving tips that all good waiters have used at some point:

1. Write **"thank you"** on your guests' checks. Studies show that it can increase your tips by 13%.

2. **Speak to your guests**, learn their preferences, and suggest drinks, appetizers, entrees, and desserts. Try to sell the experience!

3. Always **stay positive** and approach guests with a **smile.**

4. Offer recommendations to guests based on their preferences and your experiences.

5. Try to remember the guest's names and faces. If they become a repeat customer and you remember your name, guests will be blown away.

6. Know your restaurant's VIPs.

7. Always **actively listen** to your guests.

8. **Smile at every guest** you make eye contact with.

9. Try to not interrupt a guest's conversation.

10. Handle glasses by the stems and plates by the bottoms. Basically, never touch the surface area that a guest will come in contact with.

11. **Never say "I don't know"**. If you actually don't know the answer, respond with "let me find out".

12. Never remove a plate with food on it without asking a guest first. And if a guest asks you to take it, ask what was wrong with the dish.

13. Never swear in front of your guests, unless your restaurant's theme is like Dick's Last Resort Restaurant, "an American restaurant chain renowned for its obnoxious waiting staff... all in the name of fun."

14. **Be consistent** with your service throughout every course.

15. Never let a guest over-order. Offer advice and let them know portion sizes in advance.

16. **Don't ignore a table just because it isn't in your section**. If you see someone who needs help, do. Your colleagues will love you for it.

17. Don't leave place settings if they aren't going to be used.

18. Let guests know if the kitchen or bar is out of something as soon as possible so they don't read it on the menu and get disappointed.

19. If one of your guests asks to speak to a manager, don't take it personally.

20. Always place the check in a neutral place. Otherwise, you risk letting your personal biases show, which isn't good.

21. Learn your restaurant's **point of sale system** like it's the back of your hand. It's your go-to tool for managing a service.

Matthew 20:28 says, "Just as the Son of Man did not come to be served, but to serve, and to give HIS life as a ransom for many."

Matthew 5:17 says that JESUS, knowing that the Father had given all things into HIS hands and that HE had come from GOD and was going back to GOD, declared, "I did not come to **abolish** (formally put an end to) the law but to fulfill."

In other words, HE did not come to disregard what was done before but to offer salvation.

JESUS serves and works at the time other people typically relax: after supper. But HE gets comfortable for an uncomfortable act. We see a wonderful Savior preparing for an act of kindness, which can also be viewed by some as a disgusting act. My question to you is how do you view JESUS when HE is in cleaning mode? Typically, when JESUS is nasty, we are usually clean.

According to John 13:4, JESUS rose from supper. HE laid aside HIS outer garments, and, taking a towel, tied it around HIS waist. Then HE poured water into a basin and began to wash the disciples' feet and to wipe them with the towel that was wrapped around HIM.

HE wiped their feet with the towel after HE washed them with

HIS hands. But in order for this to be done, HE (the Master) bowed down to the disciple, and in HIS bowing, we see the physical position change from Savior to Server._

HE came to Simon Peter, who said to HIM, "LORD, do you wash my feet?" JESUS answered him, "What I am doing you do not understand now, but afterward you will understand."

Every now and then we all need a "present-moment non-understanding act" so that we can have an "afterwards appreciation". Those are the times when it hits you. They can be the weirdest times, but pay mind to reflect on why you survived what you survived, on how you made it out of what you were stuck in.

In the same passage in John, Peter said to JESUS, "You shall never wash my feet." JESUS answered him, "If I do not wash you, you have no share with me."

In other words, JESUS says, "Peter, if you don't let me touch the dirtiest part of your body and transfer your dirt to My hands, then I will defeat and disregard My purpose."

CHRIST JESUS Came to Save Sinners

1 Timothy 1:12-16 (ESV) says, "I thank HIM who has given me strength, CHRIST JESUS our LORD, because HE judged me faithful, appointing me to HIS service, though formerly I was a blasphemer, persecutor, and insolent opponent. But I received mercy because I had acted ignorantly in unbelief, and the grace of our LORD overflowed for me with the faith and love that are in CHRIST JESUS. The saying is trustworthy and deserving of full acceptance, that CHRIST JESUS came into the world to save sinners, of whom I am the foremost. But I received mercy for this

reason, that in me, as the foremost, JESUS CHRIST might display HIS perfect patience as an example to those who were to believe in HIM for eternal life.

John 13:9-11 says, "Simon Peter said to HIM, 'LORD, not my feet only but also my hands and my head!' JESUS said to him, 'The one who has bathed does not need to wash, except for his feet, but is completely clean. And you are clean, but not every one of you...'"

He knew who was to betray HIM; that was why HE said, "Not all of you are clean."

The passage continues (John 13:12-17): "When HE had finished washing their feet, HE put on HIS clothes and returned to HIS place. 'Do you understand what I have done for you?' HE asked them. 'You call ME Teacher and LORD, and rightly so, for that is what I am. Now that I, your LORD and Teacher, have washed your feet, you also should wash one another's feet. I have set you an example that you should do as I have done for you. Very truly I tell you, no servant is greater than his master, nor is a messenger greater than the one who sent him. Now that you know these things, you will be blessed if you do them.'"

We should be of **service** to at least three critical entities:

1. **GOD**

   o   1 Samuel 12:24 says, "But be sure to fear the LORD and serve HIM faithfully with all your heart; consider what great things HE has done for you."

   o   John 12:26 says, "Whoever serves me must follow me; and where I am, my servant also will be. My Father will honor the one who serves me."

Question: Do you give HIM your best service? Are you as faithful to HIM as you should be? Why or why not? Is your service to HIM routine, ritual, or radical?

2. <u>Church</u>

o   You can volunteer, pray, and share your gift with others.

o   Pray for yourself, your church, your pastor and his family

o   Serve by sharing your gift and your seed.

Question: What is your gift? What is it that others gain from you that benefits them? What is the thing or the reason that causes you to wake up before the alarm clock goes off? Do you really give to the church like you should? Can you really do better? Is the LORD priority on your "giving" list or only on your "asking" list?

Ephesians 2:10 says, "For we are HIS workmanship, *created* in CHRIST JESUS for good works, which GOD prepared beforehand, that we should walk in them."

"For we are HIS" – That's enough to shout about.

"Workmanship" – We are HIS product, we are HIS Fabric.

"Created" – form, shape, to completely change or transform.

From *creation* is where we get the idea of proprietorship.

Proprietorship: the state or right of owning a business or holding property.

"The company was established in 1912 and is still under the proprietorship of the same family."

Alternate definition: a business or property, etc., owned by a proprietor.

"Plenty of new firms, especially sole proprietorships, don't make money in their first few years of operation."

"Good works" – Good deeds. What are some "good deeds" as they relate to serving others?

1. Smile

2. Hold the door open

3. Give an honest compliment

4. Thank someone who you appreciate

5. Be a good listener

6. Offer your help to someone

7. Ask the person who's serving you how their day is going

8. Treat someone to a coffee or tea

9. Let someone go past you in the grocery queue

10. Send flowers or chocolates to a friend out of the blue

Psalms 100:3 says, "Know ye that the LORD HE *is* GOD: *it is* HE *that* hath made us, and not we ourselves; *we are* HIS people, and the sheep of HIS pasture."

Romans 14:7-9 (NIV) says, "For none of us lives for ourselves alone, and none of us dies for ourselves alone. If we live, we live for the LORD; and if we die, we die for the LORD. So, whether we live or die, we belong to the LORD. *Hallelujah!*"

Isaiah 43:1 (ESV) says, "**Fear** not, for I have *redeemed* you; I have called you by name, you are mine.

Redeemed: to be bought back, regain possession; delivered from sin.

2 Corinthians 5:17-19 (ESV) says, "Therefore, if anyone is in CHRIST, he is a new creation. The old has passed away; behold, the new has come. All this is from GOD, who through CHRIST reconciled us to HIMSELF and gave us the ministry of reconciliation; that is, in CHRIST GOD was reconciling the world to HIMSELF, not counting their trespasses against them, and entrusting to us the message of reconciliation."

Reconciliation is the Greek word katallagē, meaning "an exchange; reconciliation, restoration to favor."

3. <u>Community</u>

o   Proverbs 19:17 says, "Whoever is kind to the poor lends to the LORD, and HE will reward them for what they have done."

o Philippians 2:4 says not to look to our own interests, but each of us to the interests of the others.

Question: Do you keep your community up or clean? What does your community gain by having you there? Do you share the gospel with your neighbors? Do your neighbors know if you are saved? Can they tell by your lifestyle?

BONUS (Yourself)

2 Chronicles 15:7 says, "But as for you, be strong and do not give up, for your work will be rewarded."

So now, why is serving or being a servant so important?

o It shows your supportive side when it's not your season. (Observe and learn. Sometimes it's a free lesson.)

o You shine outside of the main spotlight so that when it's time to shine, you've already been acquainted with light.

o It shows commitment to the task.

o Serving builds the Kingdom Of GOD, and when HIS Kingdom is being built, HE is pleased.

o Serving allows us to witness firsthand the Savior's hand. Serving HIM puts us all in the second seat.

o Servanthood births determination.

o Serving creates a spirit of excellence and success.

o Serving keeps us humble.

o Serving GOD is a position that you are qualified for by

serving others. Serve laterally before you vertically. Serving goes out, then up, and HIS blessing come down and then out.

o   Serving will naturally change your language from "me" to "we".

o   Serving can boost your self-esteem.

o   Serving can be contagious.

o   Serving gives us purpose and meaning.

o   Serving connects us to others and allows us to be proud of ourselves.

SERVICE and SERVANTS in Scripture

Luke 5:17-20 tells a story of a man with "palsy", a medical term that refers to different types of paralysis: weakness, loss of feeling, or uncontrolled body movement.

o   Verse 17 mentions pharisees and doctors...but also the power of the LORD.

o   Verse 18 mentions men (friends?) and palsy.

o   Verse 19 mentions creating a path and push.

o   Verse 20 mentions a palsy being healed by the presence of the faith of others and the power of the LORD.

According to Philippians 2:19-22, Timothy is a servant to Paul. The servanthood Timothy has for Paul is what got him promoted.

Awesome teachers were good students.

Look at the major themes of the book of Timothy based off his service:

5 Mega Themes from 1 Timothy:

1. Sound doctrine.

2. Public worship.

3. Church leadership.

4. Personal discipline.

5. A caring church.

4 Mega Themes from 2nd Timothy:

1. Boldness.

2. Faithfulness.

3. Preaching/teaching.

4. Error.

Joshua 1:1-2 says that Moses died and Joshua was blessed with position and possession.

Verses 2 and 7 describe Moses as "servant" although his job was to lead people.

Verse 13 references "Moses the servant".

Verse 15 references "Moses the LORD's servant".

Verses 6 and 9 describe how the LORD gave Joshua advice on how to handle the main seat after being faithful in the second seat. In the second seat, you are usually faithful to GOD and to the person in the first seat, but in the second seat, you are faithful to GOD and all the people you are commanded to watch over. It's easy and tough (sometimes) to be faithful to GOD. It's always tough to be faithful to people you have to watch over. The people might not always show up, but the leader has to show up. The people might not always feel like dealing with certain issues from others, but the leader's main responsibility is dealing with people and issues. The people might give tithes and offerings (especially this time of year), but the leader has to give their time, money, and energy.

This is why the LORD gives the powerful advice for Joshua in verses 6 and 9 to be strong and of good courage.

My question now becomes: Where do I find strength when leadership and ministry make me weak?

Psalms 46:1 says, "GOD is our refuge and strength."

That word "refuge" literally means HE is my shelter from danger. In other words, HE is my safe place.

Psalms 27:4-5 describes more coverage from danger, saying: "One thing I have asked of the LORD; this is what I desire: to dwell in the house of the LORD all the days of my life, to gaze on the beuty of the LORD and seek HIM in HIS temple. For in the day of trouble HE will hide me in HIS shelter; HE will conceal me under the cover of HIS tent; HE will set me high upon a rock."

Look up! Psalms 121: 1-2 says it best: "I will lift up mine eyes to the hills, from whence cometh my HELP. My help come from the LORD, which made Heaven and Earth."

Ephesians 6:10 says, "Finally, be strong in the LORD and the power of HIS might." (**might:** ability/force or strength)

Now my question becomes: Where is courage or encouragement?

My encouragement is in Deuteronomy 31:6 – "Be strong and courageous. Do not be afraid or terrified because of them, for the LORD your GOD goes with you: HE will never leave you nor forsake you."

Psalms 23: 5-6 says, "You prepare a table before me in the presence of my enemies. You anoint my head with oil; my cup overflows. Surely Your goodness and love will follow me all the days of my life, and I will dwell in the house of the LORD forever."

1 Samuel 30:6 says, "And David was greatly distressed; for the people spoke of stoning him, because the soul of all the people was grieved, every man for his sons and daughters; but David encouraged himself in the LORD his GOD."

Chapter

WE MUST BE A CHURCH OF GIVERS AND TITHERS

A. Throughout the Bible, we discover the importance, significance, and value in "giving". As we enter into a season of purpose and expectancy from our Heavenly Father, we must enter it knowing that GOD expects us to be faithful with our giving. It is important to give because we are instructed to. I personally GIVE for three reasons: <u>obedience</u>, <u>expectancy</u>, and <u>unselfishness</u>. Anything we do, we must make sure that our hearts are aligned with heaven. It is vital that we understand as givers, and because we are blessed, that the giving of anything to the LORD, or because of the LORD, is a serious matter.

Here's an analogy:

You go to school or to job for an honest day's work. You work hard and pour your time and energy into that job because you want to earn your pay and possibly be promoted. You have to deal with various personalities, characteristics, attitudes, behaviors, kinds of conduct, levels of laziness, and situations where you're in crunch time. You get off, and you are exhausted, tired, and beat, and feel useless. But you still have to get the kids to practice and get home to cook. By the end of the day, your feet hurt, you are dreaming of how your bed will feel, and the only rational thought you have is relaxing.

You get home and find out that a back window is busted, and an intruder has been in your home. You walk around and notice you extra money is gone, your computer is gone, your kid's rooms have been ransacked, clothes are missing, purses are missing, kids toys are missing. You have been robbed! You feel wrong in your own house, you are feeling several different emotions at the same time. You feel hurt, useless, wronged, betrayed, angry, sad, raged and concerned all together.

Whenever we fail to give GOD what is HIS, that's exactly how HE feels.

Let us look into Malachi 3:8-18 (Old Testament law).

We will look at two things robbing GOD and our words. Speaking harshly is mentioned in verse 13. So basically we are looking at withholding what's HIS and our attitude.

The question now becomes: Do we give out of love or law? Do we give forcefully or freely? Do we give to dangerously or delightfully? Do we give bountifully or boastfully? Do we give angrily or anxiously?

2 Cor. 9:6-19 describes giving to support those in ministry.

1 Cor. 16:2 mentions putting aside a portion of what you earned during the week. (The emphasis is on "portion".)

Mark 12:41-44 says to give trustworthy and with good intentions and that all the rich people gave a small portion of their abundance, and the poor widow came and gave her all.

Acts 2:44-45 says that all the believers came together and sold their possessions to help the needy.

We are blessed to be a blessing. So, not only should our hearts be aligned with heaven as *instructional*, but our hearts should be aligned to one another as *relational* so that we can remain *functional*.

As we reflect back on our sermon from Sunday, we see the benefits of giving our energy. Genesis 24:15-25 describes the prayer of the servant, the willingness of the young lady, the giving of the young lady, her effort and energy to make sure the servant was hydrated with only having one jar for him and ten camels.

It is a requirement for us to give (if we are believers who trust HIM).

We should be obedient enough to give. Giving is a form of obedience and our proof of love to CHRIST. HE has blessed us, so in return we should be obedient and bless HIM. He deserves everything we possess, but because of who HE is, HE only allows us to give HIM a tent. This is a place for us to be grateful that we do not serve a selfish GOD but rather serve a sovereign GOD.

There is a certain way for us to give (being cheerful givers). Our attitudes and our hearts should be right and pure as we (or before we) approach GOD with our gifts.

Ephesians 4:31-32 (TLB) says, "Stop being mean, bad-tempered, and angry. Quarreling, harsh words, and dislike of others should have no place in your lives. Instead be kind to each other, tenderhearted, forgiving one another, just as GOD has forgiven you because you belong to CHRIST."

If GOD would allow Paul to share the importance of unity in the Spirit as it relates to loving one another with our attitudes, then surely when we approach HIM, our attitudes must be right.

o   We should give with energetic attitudes.

o   We should give with determined attitudes.

o   We should give with exciting attitudes.

o   We should give with motivating attitudes.

o   We should give with mature attitudes.

o   We should give with sincere attitudes.

o   We should give with trusting attitudes.

o   We should give with serious attitudes.

o   We should give with humble attitudes.

o   We should give with willing attitudes.

o   We should given with expecting attitudes.

o   We should give with devoted attitudes.

o   We should give with focused attitudes.

Giving can bless our futures. Abram's future was blessed because he gave GOD trust and a "yes". All of this was done because when GOD told him to leave his country after the death of his father, he left (Genesis 12:1-4).

Genesis 13:1 shows that Abram was still on the move.

Genesis 13:14-18 details the LORD explaining what all will belong to him, and he builds GOD an altar.

Genesis 15:2-6 references "I have no son... Look at the stars."

Genesis 16:1-3 says that Sarai gave her handmaid Hagar to Abram to have a child, but it was not the promised child.

Genesis 17:1-4 details that GOD told Abram, "If you obey Me, I'll make a covenant (contract) with you that will multiply you and make you a mighty nation."

Several scriptures prove the importance and the benefits of giving:

Acts 20:32-35 (TLB) says, "And I now entrust you to GOD and HIS care to HIS wonderful Word, which are able to build your faith and give you all the inheritance of those who are set apart for HIMSELF. I have never been hungry for money or fine clothing. You know that these hands of mine worked to pay my own way and even to supply the needs of those who were with me. And I was a constant example to you in helping the poor; for I remembered the words of the LORD JESUS, 'It is more blessed to give than to receive.'"

John 3:16 says, "For GOD so loved the world that HE gave HIS only begotten SON, that whosoever believeth in HIM should not perish, but have everlasting life."

Matthew 14:13-21 details the story of the 5,000 fed with two fish and five loaves of bread with twelve baskets full left over.

Acts 3:6 says, "Then Peter said, 'Silver and gold have I none but such as I have give I thee: in the name of JESUS CHRIST of Nazareth rise up and walk.'"

o   JESUS gave sight.

o   JESUS gave love.

o   JESUS gave life (Lazarus).

o   JESUS gave up the ghost.

There is even a connection to our health and wellness, as they are tied to our giving. Giving makes us feel good. It decreases blood pressure. 2 Corinthians 9:6-7 says, "GOD loves a cheerful giver."

If we want GOD to see the seriousness of our hearts, we must be willing to release what we treasure from our hands.

Chapter

8

WE MUST BE A CHURCH OF EDUCATION

We must understand as a body of believers that it is very important to have a knowledge of our Bible and what is within it. In regard to education of the Bible, we might not see the words "elementary", "middle school", "high school", or "college", but we will see words such as "rabbi", "master", "leader", "train", "teacher", "student", "knowledge", "wisdom", and even the word "study".

Romans 12:2 says, "And be not conformed to this world: but be ye transformed by the renewing of your mind, that ye may prove what is that good, and acceptable, and perfect, will of GOD."

The Living Bible translation puts it this way: "Don't copy the behavior and customs of this world but be a new and different person with a fresh newness in all you do and think. Then you will learn from your own experience how HIS ways will satisfy you."

I believe that experience can sometimes be the best teacher we have.

I typed a search in Google about things we can learn from experience, and I landed on The Thought Catalog site.

It is my personal belief that you do not need to have a degree to preach GOD's word; however, to teach it in its context will take further study. We cannot afford to be ignorant to the Word of GOD because of our laziness in diving deeper or beyond the surface of scripture.

It is also my personal belief that if GOD is revealing a fresh word to the preacher, and you are declaring what HE said, then you are educated to a point because you are revealing HIS relevant Word. We get in trouble when we get GOD's Word confused with our word or agenda.

Wisdom: the quality of having experience, knowledge, and good judgment; the quality of being wise.

In other words, it is my personal belief that experience counts for something.

If we are going to teach CHRIST, HE must be our top priority.

We cannot teach what we do not know.

GOD wants the world to learn of HIM, know HIM, learn of HIS power, know HIS power, learn of HIS blessings, know HIS blessing, learn of creation, know HIS creation, learn of HIS purpose, know HIS purpose, learn of HIS love, know HIS love, learn of HIS ways, know HIS ways. You cannot spell "knowledge", "knowledgeable", or "acknowledge" without spelling "know".

Knowledge: facts, information, and skills acquired by a person through experience or education; the theoretical or practical understanding of a subject.

Knowledgeable: intelligent, well-informed.

Acknowledge: accept or admit the existence or truth of.

2nd Timothy 2:15 says, "Study to show thyself approved unto GOD, a workman that needeth not to be ashamed, rightly dividing the word of truth."

Paul takes up the title of spiritual father/mentor to a young Timothy in some important lessons.

The word "study" would suggest or lead one to expect to "learn" of what is being presented.

"Study" is defined as the devotion of time and attention to acquiring knowledge on an academic subject, especially by means of books.

President of Harvard University Derek Bok says, "If you think education is expensive, try ignorance."

Charles Spurgeon said, "Where the plough does not go, and the seed is not sown, the weeds are quite sure to multiply; and if children are left untutored and untrained, all sorts of evils will spring up in their hearts and lives."

Malcolm X said, "Education is the passport to the future, for tomorrow belongs to those who prepare for it today."

My question for you today is: What do you know? What are you prepared for? How often do you study the Word? What does your library consist of? How important is JESUS to you? What more do you know about HIM, HIS works, HIS enemies, HIS friends and family? How much time do you really give HIM? Is GOD really first in your life? Prove it!

Proverbs 22:6 says, "Train up a child in the way he should go; even when he is old, he will not depart from it."

Proverbs 23:22 says, "Listen to your father who gave you life, and do not despise your mother when she is old."

Titus 2:4 says, "And so train the young women to love their husbands and children."

Chapter

WE MUST BE A CHURCH OF SPIRITUAL AWARENESS

Spiritual Awareness: the consciousness of spiritual matters.

For lack of better terms, it is being aware of all things spiritual.

Matthew 17:14-21 (TLB) says:

"When they arrived at the bottom of the hill, a huge crowd was waiting for them. A man came and knelt before JESUS and said, 'Sir, have mercy on my son, for he is mentally deranged, and in great trouble, for he often falls into the fire or into the water; so I brought him to your disciples, but they couldn't cure him.' JESUS replied, 'Oh, you stubborn, faithless people! How long shall I bear with you? Bring him here to Me.'" Then JESUS rebuked the demon in the boy and it left him, and from that moment the boy was well. Afterwards the disciples asked JESUS privately, 'Why couldn't we cast the demon out?' 'Because of your little faith,' JESUS told them. 'For if you had faith even as small as a tiny mustard seed you could say to this mountain, 'Move!', and it would go far away. Nothing would be impossible. But this kind of demon won't leave unless you have prayed and gone without food."

o **Verse 15:** This man's son was mentally deranged, which means his mind was not functioning at normal capacity. It was so bad that he would fall into fire or water, which means he was dealing with either burn problems or breathing problems. When you have been burnt long enough or bad enough, you lose feeling due to dead skin and cells. The devil wants you numb or not breathing at all.

o **Verse 16:** The father takes his son to JESUS' circle, which is one of the first signs of spiritual awareness: recognizing a problem and not finding excuses to hide it or cover it up. The father recognized that his son was battling something that he couldn't handle, so he sat his pride down and sought help. Now, yes, the father should have prayed against the matter, but let's appreciate the fact that he didn't keep the problem secluded. The sad part is that the disciples, who walked, talked, and ate with JESUS were so sadly dependent upon HIM that they didn't realize that they possessed the same power as JESUS. If you are going to evaluate spiritual awareness, you need to be spiritual enough to know what you possess and how to work it.

o **Verse 17:** JESUS basically says that some of us are so stubborn and rebellious that we forget to activate our faith. "But since your faith bring to me…because in my presence you cant leave like you came."

o **Verse 18:** JESUS rebukes the demon. Another aspect of spiritual awareness is facing your demons head on. And the result of JESUS attacking it head-on was that the demon left the boy at that moment, and he was well.

o **Verses 19, 20, and 21:** JESUS basically tells them, "Your problem is your little faith... You have to approach satanic attacks with spiritual approaches." JESUS says in verse 21: "This kind of demon". This would suggest to us that we should be aware of Satan's demons and plans. This was a mental problem, which attacked his mind, but it could be a relationship demon, a sickness demon, a financial demon, a generational demon, and so on.

This is why you must know how to guard yourself and fight. Because the devil and his army are closer than you think.

"Then there was war in heaven; Michael and the angels under his command fought the Dragon and his hosts of fallen angels. And Dragon lost the battle and was forced from heaven. This great Dragon – the ancient serpent called the devil, or Satan, the one deceiving the whole world – was thrown down onto the earth with all his army." (Revelation 12:7-9)

Verses 13-17 make it clear that if the devil can't have you, he will take your children.

Mark 5:1-20 Highlights:

o **Verse 5:** Ruin yourself.

o **Verse 6:** Recognition of the sovereign.

o **Verse 9:** Raging of the spirit(s). Violent and forceful.

o **Verse 10:** Regional. Some spirits hang in certain areas/ regions.

o **Verses 11-13:** Release and transfer of spirits...by command (power of words) must be bold.

o **Verse 19:** JESUS resends the man back home.

o **Verse 20:** Restart, refreshed for a new purpose. The man is now bragging and proclaiming the works of JESUS CHRIST.

Mark 5:1-20 Full Scripture – Healing of a Demoniac:

"So they came to the other side of the lake, to the region of the Gerasenes. Just as JESUS was getting out of the boat, a man with an unclean spirit came from the tombs and met HIM. He lived among the tombs, and no one could bind him anymore, not even with a chain. For his hands and feet had often been bound with chains and shackles, but he had torn the chains apart and broken the shackles in pieces. No one was strong enough to subdue him. Each night and every day among the tombs and in the mountains, he would cry out and cut himself with stones. When he saw JESUS from a distance, he ran and bowed down before HIM. Then he cried out with a loud voice, 'Leave me alone, JESUS, Son of the Most High GOD! I implore you by GOD – do not torment me!' (For JESUS had said to him, "Come out of that man, you unclean spirit!") JESUS asked him, 'What is your name?' And he said, 'My name is Legion, for we are many.' He begged JESUS repeatedly not to send them out of the region. There on the hillside, a great herd of pigs was feeding. And the demonic spirits begged HIM, 'Send us into the pigs. Let us enter them.' JESUS gave them permission. So the unclean spirits came out and went into the pigs. Then the herd rushed down the steep slope into the lake, and about 2,000 were drowned in the lake. Now the herdsmen ran off and spread the news in the town and countryside, and the people went out to see what had happened. They came to JESUS and saw the demon-possessed man sitting there, clothed and in his right mind – the one who had the 'Legion' – and they were afraid. Those who had seen what had happened to the demon-possessed man reported it, and they also told about the pigs. Then they began to beg JESUS to leave their region. As he was getting into the boat the man who had been demon-possessed asked if he could go with HIM. But JESUS did not permit him to do so. Instead, HE said to him, 'Go to your home and to your people and tell them what the LORD has done for you, that HE had mercy on you.' So he went away and began to proclaim in the Decapolis what JESUS had done for him, and all were amazed."

How to fight against demonic forces:

1.   Your actions must match your "Get thee behind me" voice.

2.   You must be bold with the power of your words.

3.   You must be disciplined about who and what you attach yourself to (spirits transfer).

How to recognize the movement of GOD: voice and actions.

What does my dream mean?

Gen 37:3-4 explains that Joseph was hated by his brothers because of the love Israel had for him being birthed at an old age. Joseph was proof that the father could still produce. In other words, if some people can't steal your existence, they won't respect your dreams. Genesis 37:5-10 makes clear that you should be careful of when and who you share your dreams with. Timing is everything.

The results of talking too soon or to the wrong person will either push you or put you under pressure. Genesis 37:18 is the proof of talking too soon; they began to plot on his life. Remember: These are his brothers, being jealous, fighting for power, fighting for position, fighting for attention, and these are very dangerous combinations. Genesis 37:23 highlights that the enemy wants to strip you of the cover that your father has given you. Genesis 39:3 details that Potiphar (Joseph's slavemaster) noticed that the LORD was with him. Genesis 39:6 proves that when you are a dream carrier, the LORD will cover the carrier. Genesis 39:6-11 is a great reminder to protect your dream status at all times. Don't fall into peer pressure.

Daniel 2:1-41

Dreams have purpose; they either reflect where you've been or where you're going. Dreams can possibly be spiritual truth. The same dream is worth looking into.

What do I do with my dreams?

o   Write down what you remember. A dream is a spiritual snapshot copy of mental visions.

o   Try to recognize symbolism or things that stand out (ex: snakes, falling, fighting, etc.) A photograph is a collection of small pieces that makes up a big picture. Dreams are collections of a big picture. (The question is: What is the picture?)

o   Pray for clarity.

How do I tap back into a place of holiness?

o   <u>Spirit of Discernment:</u> (my personal definition) spiritual eyesight to see what is unseen. In Genesis 41:33-42, Joseph had discernment.

o Proverbs 10:13 (CSB) says, "Wisdom is found on the lips of the discerning, but a rod is for the back of the one who lacks sense."

o Proverbs 16:21 (CSB) says, "Anyone with a wise heart is called discerning, and pleasant speech increase learning."

Romans 12:2 (CSB) says, "Do not be conformed to this age but be transformed by the renewing of your mind, so that you may discern what is good, pleasing, and the perfect will of GOD (divine plan for your life)."

10

WE MUST BE A CHURCH OF AUTHORITY

Matthew 28:18 (CSB) says, "JESUS came near and said to them, 'All authority has been given to me in heaven and on earth.'"

This is one of the first messages that was spoken after the resurrection of CHRIST. This is the declaration of authority and power after a plot in verses 13-15. By verse 17, the disciples worship HIM, then HE makes this declaration, and then HE gives the assignment to "go ye therefore." This is the claim of the scripture: Never accept assignment from someone who is powerless or someone who doesn't know their purpose.

Ephesians 2:6 says, "And raised us up with HIM, seated us with HIM, in the heavenly places."

Ephesians 2:10 says, "For we are HIS workmanship...creation..."

In other words, what HE has, we have.

John 14:12 says, "Verily, Verily, I say unto you, HE that believeth on Me , the works (in the Greek means actions or deeds) that I do shall HE do also; and greater works than these shall HE do; because I go unto my FATHER."

In other words, we possess it because HE passed it to us.

Proverbs 18:21 says, "Death and life are in the power of tongue, and those who love it will eat of its fruits."

In other words, your boldness is already in your body, and your power is in your mouth. On the edge of your lips is either professed pain or a pleasing promise. In other words, if all you do is complain, then your life will be dreadful, but if you see the positive in every situation, your attitude will be better.

1 John 4:1-4 (TLB) makes it clear, dear young friends, that you belong to GOD and have already won your fight with those who are against CHRIST because there is someone in your hearts who is stronger than any evil teacher in this wicked world.

This is why we must be bold and have authority in our actions and words. This world is wicked, and if we display soft character against the enemy, he will overtake us.

Luke 10:19-21 (TLB) says:

"And I have given you authority over all the power of the enemy, and to walk among serpents and scorpions and to crush them. Nothing shall injure you! However, the important thing is not that demons obey you, but that your names are registered as citizens of Heaven."

Verses 19 and 20 set up the instruction for the following scriptures because seventy more disciples had been chosen due to a heavy work load described to us in verse. The harvest was plentiful, but the laborers were few. And before we send out workers, we have to make sure that they are equipped for the task and equipped to stand up against the negativity of the task. Verse 21 teaches us that we are lambs going out amongst wolves. So somehow I need to know how to stay lamb-like enough with a bold spirit that I can defeat the wolf while remaining a lamb. What I know is that no matter how much of a lamb you are, it won't stop the wolf from being a wolf. But if I remain lamb-like enough while CHRIST remains Shepherd-like enough, the wolf won't be able to make it long enough to stand against the protection of a loving Shepherd.

REFERENCES

https://bible.knowing-JESUS.com/topics/Adoration,-Of-GOD

https://www.odditycentral.com/travel/dicks-last-resort-restaurant-would-you-like-insults-with-that.html

Made in the USA
Monee, IL
01 September 2022

12018433R00049